Spotlight on Equine Nutrition Series
Equine Cushing's Disease
Nutritional Management

Juliet M. Getty, Ph.D.

© 2013 Juliet M. Getty, Ph.D.

All Rights Reserved.

No part of this publication may be reproduced, stored in a retrieval system, or transmitted, in any form or by any means, electronic, mechanical, photocopying, recording or otherwise, without the written permission of the author.

Equine Cushing's Disease: Nutritional Management was transcribed and expanded from a teleseminar presented by Dr. Juliet M. Getty.

Transcription by Darlene J. Backer, CMT (DarleneJBacker@gmail.com).

Book design, editing and publication preparation by Elizabeth Testa, Testa Creative Associates (www.TestaCreativeAssociates.com).

ISBN-13: 978-1492147862

ISBN-10: 1492147869

Printed in the United States of America

Preface & Disclaimer

Equine Cushing's Disease—Nutritional Management is the updated and enhanced transcript of a teleseminar on the subject given by Dr. Juliet M. Getty. In offering the teleseminar in written form and with additional materials, the goal is to make it a useful, in-depth resource for any reader with an interest in Cushing's Disease.

Dr. Getty makes every effort to present the most accurate and helpful information based on her expertise and on the most reliable sources. She, her editor, transcriptionist and publisher take no responsibility for any results or damages that might be obtained from the reliance on the information and recommendations made in this book. Furthermore, the group collectively and individually takes no responsibility for the inherent risks of activities involving horses, including equine behavior changes that might result in personal injury.

Advice about nutrition, especially in the case of illness, injury, disorders, or conditions requiring medical treatment, is not intended to take the place of proper veterinary care. It may be used in conjunction with such care to facilitate healing and maintain health. The information provided by Getty Equine Nutrition, LLC is presented for the purpose of educating horse owners. Suggested feeds, supplements, and procedures are administered voluntarily with the understanding that any adverse reaction is the responsibility of the owner. Furthermore, Getty Equine Nutrition, LLC cannot be held accountable for a horse's response, whether favorable or adverse, to nutritional intervention.

This is not a verbatim transcript. Comments about technical matters relevant to the teleseminar process have been omitted, along with questions and answers off the specific topic at hand.

Mention of a specific product or brand name is not intended to imply that other companies offer inferior products. Dr. Getty means no intention of trademark infringement by the omission of the ® or ™ designation; all product names mentioned are presumed trade-protected.

Juliet M. Getty, Ph.D. is an internationally respected writer and lecturer on equine nutrition. She contributes articles frequently to various horse journals and media, and her comprehensive reference book, *Feed Your Horse Like a Horse*, has educated countless horsemen and women in the science behind sound equine feeding practices. Her informative e-newsletter, *Forage for Thought*, is read by several thousand subscribers every month; she is also available for private consultations and speaking engagements.

The *Spotlight on Equine Nutrition Series* offers these additional titles:

Aging Horse—*Helping Him Grow Old with Dignity and in Health*
Easy Keeper—*Making It Easy to Keep Him Healthy*
Equine Digestion—*It's Decidedly Different*
Joint Health—*A Nutritional Perspective*
Laminitis—*A Scientific and Realistic Approach*
Whole Foods & Alternative Feeds

Dr. Getty offers a generous serving of other equine nutrition knowledge at www.GettyEquineNutrition.com.

Introduction

Equine Cushing's Disease: Nutritional Management presents a nutritional perspective on current approaches to the disease commonly referred to simply as "Cushing's," which has the more scientific and descriptive name of pituitary pars intermedia dysfunction (PPID). In this book, I will refer to it both as Cushing's and as PPID. It is a disorder of the endocrine (pituitary) system.

This is not intended to be a veterinary presentation, although I will cover some physiology. Every horse owner should have a team of professionals addressing the health needs of his or her horse: a veterinarian, a farrier, other supporting specialties, and a nutritionist. That's where I come in. Nutrients play a critical role in the health of any living creature, so I analyze the horse's diet and put it in a holistic perspective that includes the horse's environment, his mental state, his exercise—anything that affects his overall health.

Some readers may be familiar with my resource book, **Feed Your Horse Like a Horse**. I draw on materials from it—and expand on them here. I have also updated the materials I covered in both of my Cushing's teleseminars; much of the background material (before the Questions and Answers section) consists of new or more detailed information.

Equine Cushing's disease very often involves a secondary health problem, insulin resistance or equine metabolic syndrome. I touch on the causes and solutions to this issue somewhat in these pages, but for more in-depth coverage, I refer you to my Spotlight on Equine Nutrition Series book, **Easy Keeper—Making It Easy to Keep Him Healthy.**

Physiology of Cushing's Disease

Equine Cushing's disease, PPID, is typically an age-related disorder. Many horses will develop Cushing's as they get older, but the symptoms come on so gradually, the disease often goes unrecognized. In fact, researchers in Australia evaluated the incidence of PPID and compared it to what horse owners suspected, and they found that many cases of PPID went undetected.

Usually around the age of 15 the risk becomes greater; however, younger and younger horses are developing PPID, and although it's not very common in horses under ten years of age, we do see it on occasion, which is a disturbing trend, to say the least.

PPID is a progressive disorder, meaning it gets progressively worse over time. Cushing's is not fatal in and of itself, but rather from the conditions it can lead to if left untreated, such as infections, muscle wasting, colic, and of course, laminitis. So the point here is that there is no cure, only treatment, and over time, treatment needs to get more aggressive.

Symptoms

Let's look first at the symptoms of Cushing's.

- The horse may be lethargic, perhaps not be as spunky or energetic.
- Increased thirst and more frequent urination.
- Athletic performance may decline.
- Behavioral changes: Perhaps the horse becomes more docile, or perhaps more excitable—how it changes depends on the horse.
- Hair coat changes: It can become longer and more curly. It also fails to shed appropriately—some horses go well into the summer before completely shedding. They maintain some guard hairs—the long hairs in the jugular groove, along the back of the legs, or on the chin.

- Muscle loss: Because of the hormones involved, the muscles will break down or atrophy, so you'll see a characteristic loss of muscle in the top line and the horse can become pot- bellied. Muscle loss is a common symptom.
- Immune system: The horse with PPID has a compromised immune system and so will often develop abscesses, may be more prone towards infections (i.e. skin, respiratory), may develop allergies, might be more sensitive to vaccinations, and so on.
- Eyes: The eyes may tear excessively.
- Sweating disorders: The horse may have trouble with sweating—he may sweat excessively or have patchy sweating, or he may have the opposite problem and not sweat at all or not enough (anhidrosis).
- Appetite changes and weight gain: Most of the time horses with Cushing's, even those not otherwise overweight, will have a secondary condition called equine metabolic syndrome, also known as insulin resistance. The signs of this are telltale regional fat deposits along the neck crest, above the eyes, the tail head, behind the shoulders, along the spine, and even on the sheath or the mammary region. The increased body fat disrupts proper signaling by a hormone called leptin, which creates leptin resistance, which results in the inability to feel satiated and initiates a vicious cycle: increased appetite leads to overeating, which leads to increased body fat, which disrupts a normal leptin response, which triggers the appetite further. (By the way, once the body's response to leptin is normalized, the appetite declines, and the cycle is broken. Interestingly, leptin is not influenced by a starchy meal; it is influenced by the level of body fat.)
- Laminitis: Although not a symptom, per se, certainly one of the most terrifying outcomes of Cushing's is laminitis, which is brought on by an increase of insulin from the concurrent equine metabolic syndrome or from the Cushing's itself. The hoof tissue can also become weakened from elevated blood cortisol levels.

Cushing's and Equine Metabolic Syndrome (Insulin Resistance) Differentiated

It's important to understand that equine metabolic syndrome and Cushing's are separate diseases. Equine metabolic syndrome (also known as insulin resistance) is often the precursor to Cushing's, as well as frequently its secondary companion.

Some equines are genetically predisposed toward developing insulin resistance: ponies and donkeys, plus certain breeds—Arabs and the draft breeds, to name two examples. But any horse can fall victim to it under certain circumstances.

Genetically speaking, insulin resistance is a survival mechanism that developed in horses before domestication. Horses in the wild, traveling miles for sparse feed, had to evolve with a mechanism that held on to body fat—insulin resistance. But in a domesticated circumstance, insulin resistance is the very opposite of useful to the horse; it's dangerously harmful.

Equine metabolic syndrome can exist on its own without Cushing's and can have similar symptoms (cresty neck and other abnormal fat deposits, as well as increased insulin levels); however, with Cushing's, the horse may be obese *or* underweight, have different physical signs (listed earlier) and show elevated levels of blood glucose and adrenocorticotropic hormone (ACTH). Both can lead to laminitis from elevated insulin but the reason for elevated insulin differs between the two disorders.

The horse can start out with metabolic syndrome; the increased body fat promotes oxidative stress, which in turn damages the dopamine-producing neurons in the part of the brain known at the hypothalamus, and that starts a cascade of degeneration typical in PPID.

The All-important Pituitary Gland

Let's look now at the pituitary gland and the damaging pathway of Cushing's. The pituitary gland is suspended from the hypothalamus at the base of the brain. There are three significant hormone-releasing lobes of the pituitary gland. The first one is the **pars distalis**, which secretes prolactin, endorphins, growth hormones, follicle-stimulating hormone, luteinizing hormone, and thyroid-stimulating hormone. The second lobe is the **pars nervosa**, which controls water balance by secreting the antidiuretic hormone commonly known as vasopressin; it also secretes the hormone oxytocin. And finally, there's the lobe involved with equine Cushing's, and that is the **pars intermedia**. The pars intermedia produces peptide hormones known as proopiomelanocortin peptides (POMC, for short) which include things like alpha-MSH (melanocyte stimulating hormone, responsible for skin pigmentation) and beta-endorphins (which cause relaxation and improved pain tolerance); in horses this particular lobe produces ACTH, the regulation of which is at the heart of the Cushing's problem itself.

Let's look at a normal situation where the horse is experiencing some kind of stress—maybe he's exercising intensely or has mental stress. He may be in pain, or suffering from an empty stomach (more on that later). It doesn't matter what the cause of the stress is—whenever there's some kind of stressor, the pituitary gland will release ACTH. See chart on page 7 for the *Normal Hormonal Cascade*.

The job of ACTH is to travel to the adrenal gland and tell it to produce the stress hormones cortisol and epinephrine, both of which are needed to release glucose, for energy, out of glycogen stores in the liver and muscle. For the moment, we will concentrate on cortisol.

The healthy body has a homeostatic mechanism to handle hormones: their levels can rise and fall and are maintained within a normal range. Stress stimulates the hypothalamus to release corticotropin releasing hormone (CRH). CRH signals the pituitary gland (pars intermedia) to release ACTH, which then stimulates the adrenal gland to secrete the stress-hormone known as cortisol. To bring cortisol levels back to normal, cortisol will stimulate certain neurons in the brain (hypothalamus) to produce the neurotransmitter, dopamine. Dopamine, in turn, tells the pituitary gland to stop secreting ACTH, which then causes cortisol production from the adrenal gland to subside.

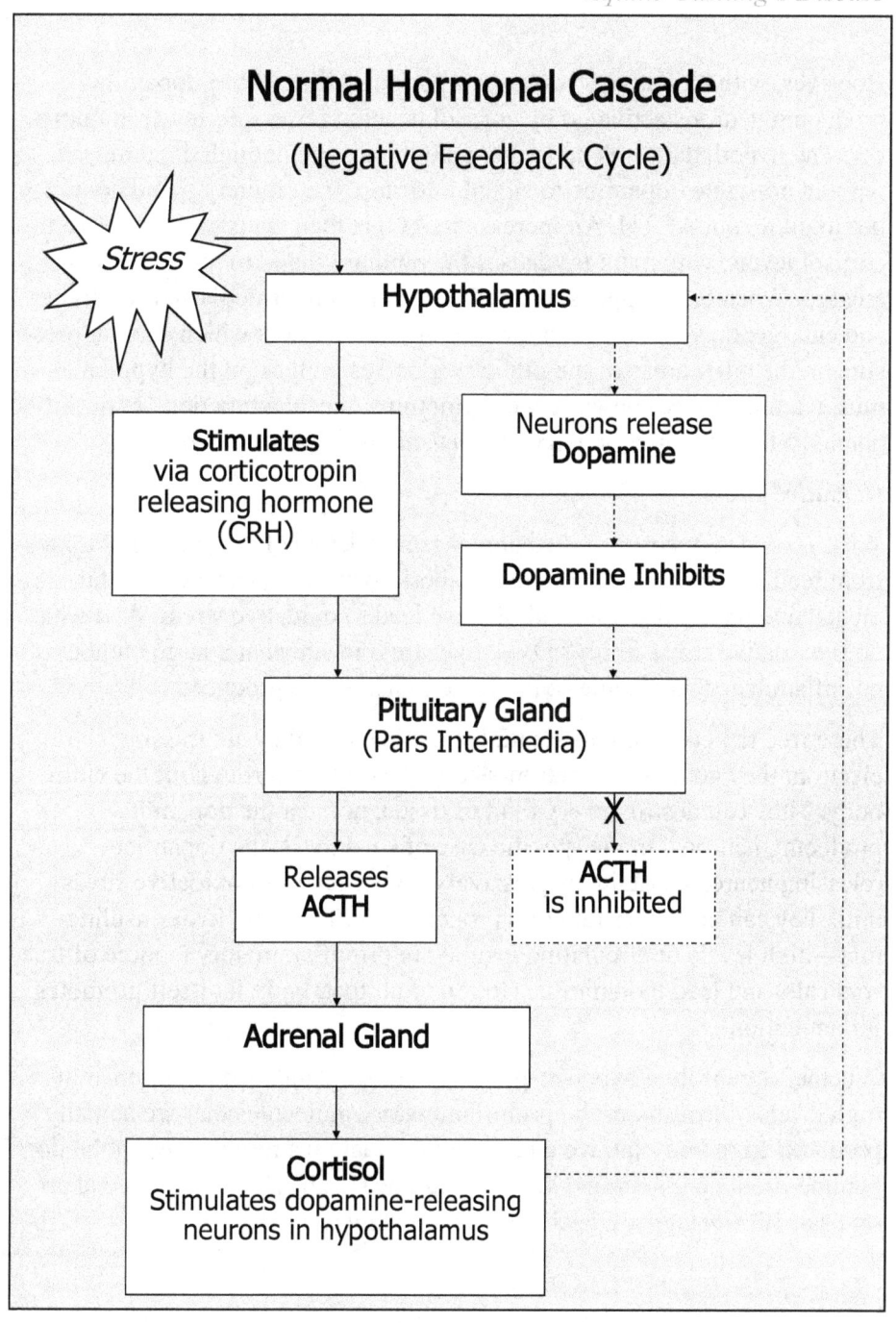

However, with oxidative stress over a period of time, those dopamine-producing neurons activated by cortisol become fewer and fewer in number. The hypothalamus is no longer able to produce enough dopamine; without adequate dopamine to signal it to stop, the pituitary gland continues to pump out ACTH. An increase in ACTH then leads to an increase in cortisol levels, which in turn causes the pituitary gland to hypertrophy or enlarge. When that happens, the cells of the pars intermedia start to divide and enlarge; they can form tumors (benign adenomas), which can put pressure on the other areas of the pituitary gland as well as on the hypothalamus, leading to a whole variety of symptoms, the "dysfunction" part of the name, PPID. See chart on page 9: *Cortisol and Oxidative Stress.*

Oxidative stress

What is oxidative stress and what makes it so lethal? Environmental toxins from feed and chemicals, equine metabolic syndrome, excess body fat, mental and physical stress—all of these lead to oxidative stress. And what does oxidative stress imply? Oxidative stress means that a large number of proinflammatory molecules called free radicals[1] are produced.

These free radicals are volatile molecules because they are missing an electron; they go on an "electron-stealing" rampage throughout the entire body. They can destroy every kind of tissue, not just the dopamine-producing neurons. In the specific case of Cushing's, the dopamine-releasing neurons sustain progressively higher levels of oxidative stress until they can no longer function properly. Furthermore, hyperinsulinemia—high levels of circulating insulin are proinflammatory (source of free-radicals) and lead to laminitis. On top of all that, body fat itself promotes inflammation.

Whether it be from a hyper-responsive adrenal gland, or the presence of high levels of insulin, or the proinflammatory molecules that are actually produced from body fat, we end up with oxidative stress damaging the dopamine-producing neurons. We have equine Cushing's disease. See chart on page 10, *Cushing's/PPID Disease Mechanism.*

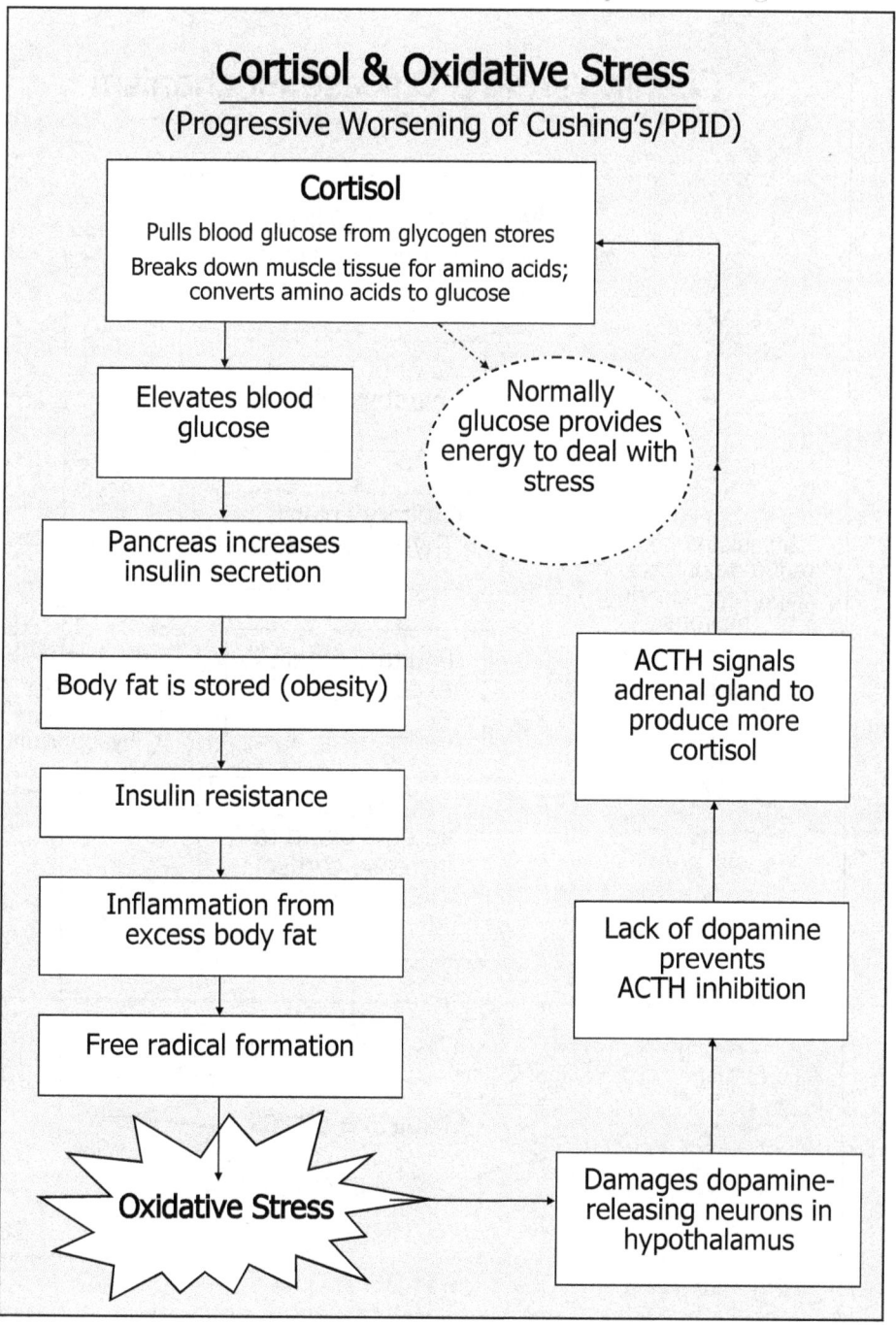

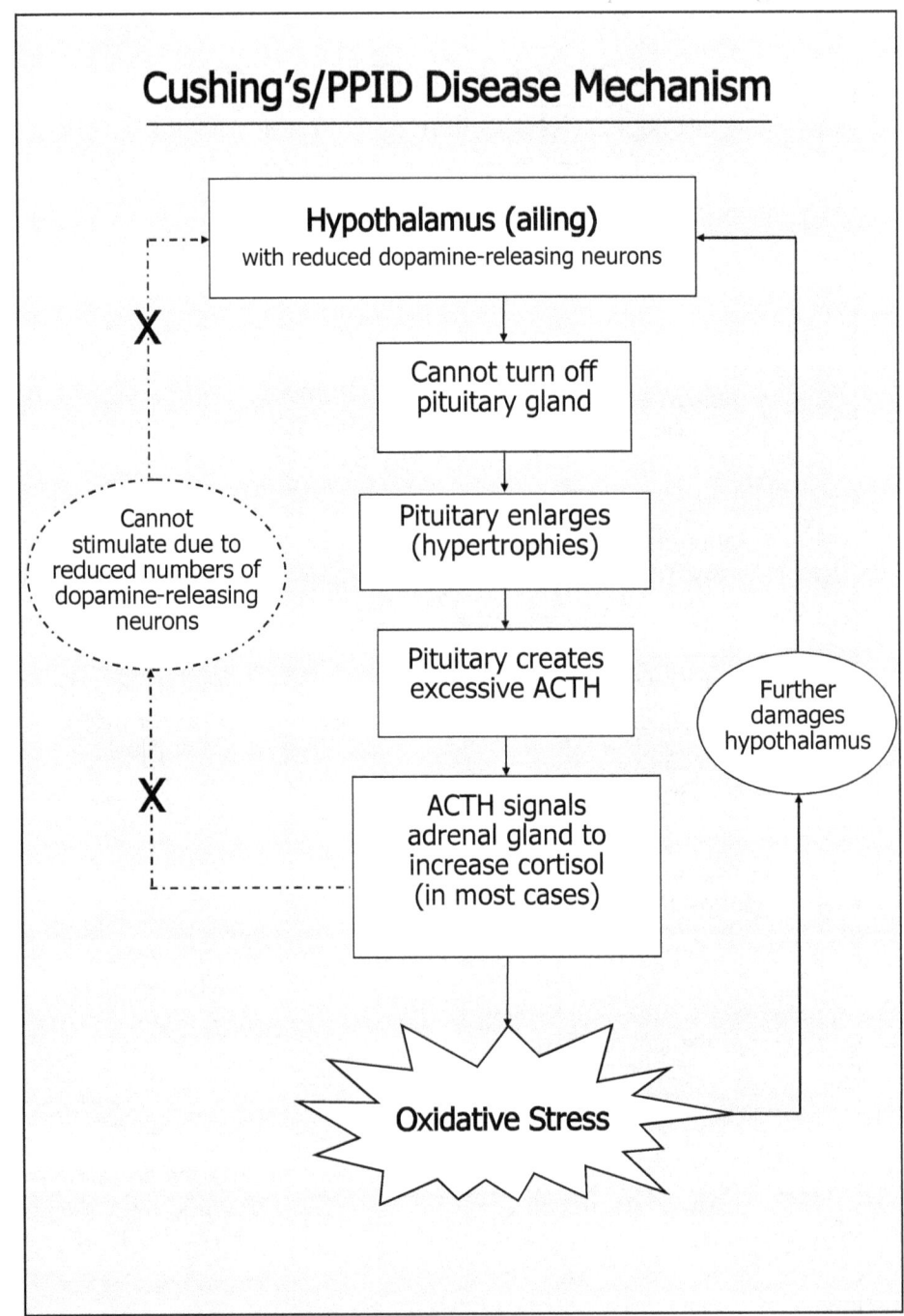

Diagnosing Cushing's

Diagnosing Cushing's is properly left to your veterinarian; however, you should be familiar with the process. Horses can start showing signs even before tests can actually confirm Cushing's, so be aware that early tests may come out negative even though the signs are there. The tests work better for more advanced cases. There is a variety of tests in use:

The **resting plasma ACTH concentration test** is the most common and best test for PPID. This can be done any time of year. We used to avoid testing during the early fall months (August, September, and October), because ACTH concentrations will be naturally higher then, leading to false-positive results. But now research has shown how to adjust the numbers for seasonal variations: between November and July, ACTH above 7.8 pmol/L (35 pg/ml) indicates PPID; between August and October, 10.4 pmol/L (47.3 pg/ml) or higher is consistent with a positive PPID diagnosis. But also understand that ACTH concentrations may be set off kilter by stress itself; remember, the pituitary responds to stress by releasing ACTH. The stressor could be simple nervousness from the presence of the veterinarian, it could be pain from an injury or laminitis, it could even be something as simple as an empty stomach. So you want your horse to be as calm and unstressed as possible for this test.

The **domperidone response test** is being used a bit more frequently now. Domperidone inhibits dopamine, and therefore ACTH will be higher in horses with PPID, but the results will be normal if the horse does not have PPID.

The **dexamethasone suppression test** is a little more involved, requiring two blood samples. If your horse is insulin resistant or has had laminitis, this test carries a risk of causing a laminitis flare-up, so vets will often shy away from it.

The **thyrotropin releasing hormone (TRH)** stimulation test is an older test for Cushing's and has a relatively high false positive result rate. In the cushingoid horse, TRH will abnormally stimulate ACTH secretion.

A **cortisol rhythm test** has often been used—this one looks for a pattern. Cortisol levels are usually lower in the evening than they are in the morning for normal horses, but that pattern is usually lost with PPID. Unfortunately, however, this test does tend to give frequent false-positives so you may want to have some other testing done.

Sometimes **insulin testing** is done, but this is tricky. Stress and pain can increase insulin resistance; just the stress of seeing the vet's truck drive up the driveway can cause insulin to get out of line.

---

[1] For more about free radicals, antioxidants, and oxidative stress, see Appendix A.

Medical Treatments for PPID

Equine Cushing's disease in most instances will eventually require pharmaceutical treatment, and the drug of choice is pergolide, but dietary management should always be implemented as a first line of defense.

Pergolide, or its trademarked version, Prascend[1], is a dopamine agonist, activating dopamine receptors in the absence of true dopamine and therefore it inhibits the production of ACTH. This helps diminish the signs of Cushing's and strengthens the body's own ability to stave off some of the disease's side effects, such as laminitis or infections. In this way, the drug can keep your horse alive a whole lot longer and in greater comfort. Some horses require Prascend or pergolide only seasonally during the times when ACTH is elevated, but most require it year round.

With pergolide use there tends to be a loss of appetite, at least in the initial stages; it can make the horse nauseated. Some horses refuse to eat. This is a very serious situation especially for ponies, donkeys, and mules because if these animals don't eat, they mobilize a lot of body fat and that can lead to a condition called hyperlipemia, which is deadly. So watch for that, please. Pergolide can also make a horse depressed.

Cyproheptadine is sometimes used, but not so commonly as pergolide; however, in advanced cases of PPID, adding cyproheptadine to Prascend can be helpful in alleviating symptoms. Trilostane is sometimes used along with pergolide to block cortisol secretion from the adrenal gland.

Most vets, however, rely on pergolide or Prascend alone.

Pain & Infection Management in Cushing's

Often the horse with PPID has some pain. Often it can be due to hoof abscesses; sometimes there is a low grade laminitis. The endorphin-producing mechanism may be impaired.

Cushing's produces elevated levels of endorphins which likely contribute to the lethargy typically experienced by these horses. Once pergolide is administered, the endorphin levels decline which may lead to increased pain intensity, especially if the horse suffers from arthritis.

Most horse owners are aware that the pain medication phenylbutazone ("bute") can lead to gastric and colonic ulcers. I have found that lecithin is protective against all ulcerations (not just those caused by bute), so if you're giving bute you want to give lecithin along with it. You can give lecithin by itself, or give it coupled with apple pectin in a product known as Starting Gate (SBS Equine Products)[2]. There is an article on lecithin in the library on my website at www.gettyequinenutrition.com.

Sometimes antibiotics may be necessary because of secondary infections. If that's the case, then make sure to give a probiotic, a potent one that also protects the immune system. For this particular situation, there are three that I find helpful: ProLactic DFM (HorseTech), Daily Start (Equi-Shine) and Synbiotic EQ (MedVet Pharmaceuticals).

---

[1] The compounding medication pergolide mesylate has been largely replaced with a drug called Prascend made by the same people that make pergolide, Boehringer Ingelheim Vetmedica. Compounding medications leave some room for error; vets may prefer the more expensive Prascend for reliability.

[2] A number of products mentioned in this teleseminar and book are carried on my website at www.gettyequinenutrition.com.

Nutrition for the Horse with Cushing's

Start with Forage

We cannot cure Cushing's, but we can work at slowing down the oxidative stress that so diminishes the health of the horse with the disease.

The first thing we want to do is make sure that your horse has forage. If you feed hay, then I recommend choosing a grass hay and offering it free choice[1]. Have your hay tested[2] to ensure that it is appropriate for the cushingoid horse.

Have the sugar and starch levels evaluated. The number you want to work with is the NSC, the nonstructural carbohydrates. This number will tell you the safety factor for your insulin resistant and/or cushingoid horse. To get that number, add the WSC (water soluble carbohydrates) in your report to percent starch[3]. (You'll have two columns; one on "as sampled" and one "dry matter." Use the "as sampled" numbers because that is what the horse is eating.) Those two numbers when added together equal NSC, and it should be less than 12 percent, ideally less than 10 percent.

Look at the calories. If your horse is overweight, the digestible energy should be no more than 0.88 Mcals (megacalories) per pound or 1.94 Mcals/kg. If your horse is not overweight, then it's not an issue.

Mineral balance is very important as well, so make sure minerals are included in the evaluation. Most forages are high in iron and this can lead to imbalances in copper, zinc, and manganese. Too much iron can also exacerbate insulin resistance. Therefore, work with an equine nutritionist to help you bring the zinc to copper ratio close to 3:1 with iron being no more than 4 times that of zinc. Manganese should also have the same ratio with copper. Mineral balancing is a service offered by Getty Equine Nutrition, LLC.

But if you cannot have your hay tested, if perhaps you get a different supply every week, then obviously testing is not reasonable. If this is the case, then you will have to soak or steam it to remove as much of the sugar that you can. To steam your hay you'll likely need to purchase a commercial hay steamer. Soak it for about 30 minutes in warm water or about an hour in cold water and then *drain the water off and discard it.* You may want to retest the hay after it has been soaked or steamed to see if the sugar/starch levels have dropped sufficiently. Something to note, though: soaking also removes a significant amount of the vitamins and the minerals so you will need to provide supplementation. Steaming removes fewer minerals and is easier to do. Refer to an article on this topic in the Library section at www.gettyequinenutrition.com

Hay should be the staple of the diet. But what if you're lucky enough to have pasture or fresh grass—can you allow your horse with Cushing's to graze? The answer is not black-and-white. Pasture grazing is not typically recommended for an insulin-resistant horse, or one that has experienced laminitis due to excessive sugar and starch intake, or one that has regional fat deposits. Keep in mind, though, that as a living tissue, grass changes all the time in sugar and starch levels (NSC) so with careful management and pasture testing[4], in some cases grazing can work successfully.

In general, if the nighttime temperatures are warm, above 40 degrees Fahrenheit, then the NSC will be lowest at dawn. On a sunny day, the grass produces sugars and starches through photosynthesis, so those levels are at their highest late in the afternoon, around five o'clock. As the sun sets, the grass begins to use the NSC it produced all day for growth, so as the NSC is depleted, the levels diminish and will be at their very lowest before dawn—early, early in the morning. And then the cycle starts again as the grass is exposed to sunlight. A good rule of thumb is "safest early in the morning; as the day gets longer, more dangerous." You could put your horses out late at night, after it's been dark for a few hours, and let them graze late at night, then take them off of pasture say around 9:30 or 10:00 in the morning, and put them into a dry lot *with a low NSC hay free choice.*

Pasture grazing management can be complex, varying widely by weather conditions. If it's a cloudy day, the grass won't produce as much sugar and starch. If it's a cold night, the grass won't relinquish the NSC so it will be higher in the morning—for example, if it goes below 40 degrees for several hours during the night, in the morning the grass will be higher in sugar and starch than if the nighttime temperature had remained warm.

You can test your pasture. Go to www.equi-analytical.com for instructions. Try to get two consecutive sunny days with nights above 40 degrees, and take your first sample on the second morning (that's your best case scenario). Then take another after the grass has been exposed to sun all day, around 5:00—that's your worst case scenario.

You will also find that as the season progresses, usually starting around late June, the NSC levels do get lower and it's safer to let your horses graze. But be careful. Once the nighttime temperatures get cold again, in the fall months, then the sugar and starch levels become higher and the risk of laminitis goes up again.

Sugar and starch levels can also become elevated anytime the grass is stressed. Drought, heavy rain, overgrazing, mowing too short (I like mowing no shorter than 4 to 6 inches), or too many weeds can cause the grass to hold on to its NSC levels.

Decreasing Insulin and Inflammation Through the Diet

The goal of nutrition management of Cushing's is to lower insulin levels.

The first approach is to feed less sugar and starch. Not only should the forage itself be low in NSC, but all cereal grains (oats, corn, barley, wheat, rice, etc.) should be avoided. Check your feed to make certain that it does not contain these. Molasses should also be avoided. Treats that contain grains and sugar are not appropriate. Fruits and carrots are also high in sugar and can be offered minimally, or not at all depending on your horse's circumstances. When giving treats, you can choose broken alfalfa cubes (if your horse does well with alfalfa) or consider Skode's horse treats, which are very low in NSC.

There are some very helpful things you can add to your horse's diet to decrease insulin. Much of what follows relies on your having a good hay analysis.

Magnesium, calcium, and chromium. There should be twice as much calcium in the diet as magnesium. Start your calculations with the level of magnesium given in your hay analysis; divide that in half because magnesium is not very well absorbed so you can assume the horse is not getting the full amount shown in the analysis. Then supplement enough magnesium to get close to half of the calcium, no more than 5000 mg/250 pounds of body weight.

Chromium can be safely supplemented. While the exact levels have not been determined, a safe range is 1 to 2 mg per 250 lbs of body weight, especially where alkaline soils lead to poor chromium uptake by grasses.

Lipoid acid. This is an antioxidant and it also lowers circulating insulin levels. Carb-X (Med-Vet Pharmaceuticals) contains lipoic acid as well as an herb called *Gymnema sylvestre*, which has been shown to lower circulating insulin levels.

Psyllium. This is not just for sand colic. Psyllium actually lowers blood glucose levels. Feed at about a third cup per meal—it will help a great deal.

Omega 3s. Omega 3s are found in ground flaxseed, chia seeds. They also lower circulating insulin levels. Fish oils are also very high in omega 3s, however, since horses are not fish-eaters, I reserve feeding fish oil for situations where there is a high level of inflammation. Keep in mind that oils that are high in omega 6s (such as soybean, corn, and wheat germ oils) have no benefit on insulin levels and increase inflammation.

Curcumin. This is the fabulous active ingredient in the spice called turmeric. CurOst (Nouvelle Veterinary Research Inc.) has some very nice preparations that contain curcumin. Also you can buy turmeric in bulk.

Vitamins E and C. I recommend high levels of these antioxidants: 5,000 IU of vitamin E for a full-sized horse (approximately 1100 lbs or

500 kgs) and vitamin C at about 10-20 mg/pound of body weight (which means if your horse weighs 1000 pounds, you would give between 10,000 and 20,000 mg of vitamin C a day).

A cautionary note: Since vitamin C increases iron absorption, before supplementing, it is worthwhile to test the blood ferritin level to see if your horse is storing excess iron (which exacerbates insulin resistance).

Tyrosine. This is an amino acid that is found in some products to treat anhidrosis, but tyrosine also promotes dopamine production and so it's worth a try; in adding tyrosine to the horse's diet, give about 1000 mg a day.

Chasteberry. Chasteberry is an herb which, along with jiaogulan, has been shown to increase dopamine levels. Studies done with humans reveal that chasteberry has a positive impact on increasing dopamine production. However, with horses there have been mixed results. It may be worth a try for a horse that is not in the advanced stages of Cushing's. There's a product that I like called Balance EQ (Foxden Equine) developed by Dr. Melyni Worth. Balance EQ at a double dose seems to be effective but you have to give it for a period of months to see if it has the same effect as the pergolide does.

Whole Foods. Some whole foods are excellent for the insulin resistant horse. Mushrooms strengthen the immune system. Other helpful foods high in antioxidants are noni juice, bilberry juice, and blueberries. CurOst offers an excellent preparation containing these three ingredients.

Carrier Meals

If you have an overweight horse that's cushingoid, then you want to add some of those supplements—but what do you add them to? You use a low starch carrier. Try beet pulp—find the kind without molasses, or if you can't get that, then soak the beet pulp and drain off the water to remove the sugar. In fact, since beet pulp is also high in iron, it is a good idea to soak and drain, even if you have the unsweetened variety. Hay pellets work well—timothy or alfalfa (if your horse can tolerate alfalfa). Alfalfa is generally lower in NSC than grasses and boosts the overall protein quality (which is important for immune function and new tissue growth). Most horses tolerate it well, but some horses are sensitive to alfalfa.

There are some low NSC commercial feeds; let me just mention a few brand names. In the January 2013 issue of the *Horse Journal*, I evaluated several different feeds and identified the ones with low NSC—under 10%. If your horse is of normal weight or is underweight, then you can give these feeds at higher levels (according to directions) to boost his calories, but if he's overweight then you'll want to feed just a little bit (or just use the carriers previously mentioned).

The five lowest NSC commercial feeds I found are in the table below.

Product	% NSC
Equi-Pro Carb Safe (Poulin Grain)	6.6
Carb-Guard (Blue Seal)	8
Stabul (NuZu Feed)	8.8
Triple Crown Safe Starch (Triple Crown Feed)	9
Triple Crown Lite (Triple Crown Feed)	9.3

Protein Quality

Protein is a clever nutrient in its ability to apply itself to the tissues as needed, but the protein level cited on a hay analysis doesn't actually tell us a whole lot about its ability to do that. It's the amino acid content within the protein that matters— amino acids will go into the bloodstream and the cells will then reassemble them, or try to, to make the kinds of proteins that the cells need. In the hoof cell, amino acids make hoof protein. In an eye cell, they make eye protein; in a liver cell, liver protein, and so on. To be useful to the body, though, protein must have the right combination of amino acids in the right ratios. This is what is meant by "protein quality."

If you feed one type of protein source and it's of poor quality (doesn't have the right complement of amino acids), there won't be enough amino acids to reassemble and so there will be some left over, unusable. Since they cannot be saved for later, the leftovers end up going to the liver where they're destroyed. This can result in the production of ammonia and urea, so the horse will urinate more and his urine will be stronger smelling. That's a sign that you're not giving enough quality protein.

But did you know that left over amino acids can actually raise insulin levels? Inside the liver, the unused amino acids are broken apart – part become ammonia and then urea and excreted in the urine. And the other part, called an organic acid, gets converted to? You guessed it! It is converted to glucose—which can raise insulin levels. So you can feed a low starch, low sugar diet but if the protein quality is low, you'll still raise insulin levels.

For this reason, you want to be very careful to provide a variety of protein sources so that your horse can make the body tissues that he needs. He'll make them in order of priority. Certainly the tissues that are most important are those that keep him alive—his lungs, his brain, his heart, his liver, his kidneys. If there are usable amino acids left over, then he'll make sure that enough antibodies are produced for healthy immune function as well as for his joints, skin, and his hair, and his hooves—but those tissues that are not life essential will suffer if the diet doesn't contain enough quality protein.

An example that is directly related to the Cushing's discussion is the amino acid, tyrosine. As we've just covered, tyrosine is directly involved in the formation of dopamine which is key to regulating the pituitary and adrenal glands. Getting enough quality protein will ensure enough tyrosine.

So how do you increase protein quality? First, you want to feed a mix of grass hays, as wide a variety as you can. Grass hays include timothy, orchard, brome, Bermuda, fescue, etc.; in addition, provide alfalfa to add variety to your protein sources. However, keep in mind that since it is high in protein it's also higher in calories. The underweight horse can have a good amount of alfalfa (no more than 50% of the total hay ration);

on the other hand, the overweight horse should probably be limited to no more than two or three pounds of it a day.

Be watchful, though—in some horses (not many), alfalfa can induce laminitis. We don't really know the reason for this, however, my theory is that it may be related to the plant estrogens or phytoestrogens found in alfalfa. Whatever the reason, if your horse is sensitive to it, then by all means avoid it. And be aware that if he's sensitive to alfalfa, he's likely also sensitive to soybean meal. Soybean meal is found in a lot of different foods so pay attention to the labels to see if that may be what's causing laminitis.

Soy has long been thought to be the best plant source of protein, being close to animal protein in quality, but we now know that hulled hemp seeds (that have the outer shell removed) rival the protein quality of soy. I compared the amino acid profiles of hemp and soy and even compared them to the animal protein, whey, which is milk protein—and hemp seeds exceeded the quality of both of those[5]. So to boost protein quality, you can add hemp seeds.

Where do you find them? You can buy them at any place that sells them in bulk—I buy mine from bulkfoods.com. They're also available at another website called nuts.com. And I recently bought some from Amazon.com; that was the best price. Depending on the horse's weight, you can give anywhere from a quarter of a cup to a full cup. They are high in fat so you don't want to give too much to an overweight horse, but the protein is absolutely wonderful and they taste excellent. (They're great for you, too, by the way. If you've never tasted them, you're in for a treat—you will really enjoy them.)

Split peas are another good source of protein for your horse. These are the same kind of dried split peas you get in the grocery store to make split pea soup. They come in green and they come in yellow. Either one is fine. You can add them, for example, to soaked beet pulp or to timothy or alfalfa pellets that you add some water to. Let them moisten for a few minutes. Horses love them; about a half cup per meal is a really nice way to give your horse some more amino acids.

For the underweight horse, you'll want to add even more calories; beyond adding alfalfa, adding more fat is also important. Ground flaxseed would be good for this; you can give an underweight, full-sized horse up to two cups of ground flaxseed a day. Or try chia seeds in the same amount—these are high in omega 3s that are anti-inflammatory.

Watch out for inflammatory oils that are high in omega 6s. Remember what we discussed earlier: A horse needs some omega 6s but if they're out of balance with omega 3s, then you're promoting inflammation—and you know where that leads: to free radical formation and then oxidative stress, which is, of course, what you want to prevent or reduce. It's hard to find an oil that's 100% suitable; all of them contain some omega 6s. Rice bran oil, for example, contains about 30% omega 6s; however, most of its fatty acids come from non-inflammatory omega 9s. Stay away from soybean oil and corn oil. Coconut oil is something you might want to consider but it doesn't add as many calories as some of the other oils do; furthermore, a horse is simply not used to ingesting medium chain triglycerides such as coconut oil has; it's not natural to their metabolism so I don't like to feed coconut oil for too long. Copra meal, by the way, is made from coconuts and it has protein but it's not very high in quality. (I talk more about these things in my "Whole Foods" teleseminar, which is also available in print and recorded versions.)

Two Goals, Two Keys to Achieving Them

Our first goal is to reduce oxidative stress, so we can prevent or reduce the destruction of dopamine-promoting neurons and therefore slow down the progression of Cushing's disease in your horse. Our second goal is to prevent laminitis; as we've discussed, all cushingoid horses are candidates for laminitis, more so if they've already had one attack or if they are already insulin resistant due to equine metabolic syndrome.

To reduce oxidative stress, as we've seen, we want to keep the body fat level down and decrease insulin resistance (increase insulin sensitivity). My teleseminar and booklet on the "Easy Keeper" addresses this in greater detail, but I'll cover it briefly here, too.

The keys are actually fairly simple: feed suitable hay free choice and increase exercise.

Feed suitable hay free choice. As we've seen, many things promote stress and its cascading negative effects, but do you know what the main source of stress is for most horses? *The main source of stress is restricting forage.* Right—the very thing most people do to try to help their horse lose weight actually causes the same stress reaction that brings about body fat retention, and all its attendant problems.

I cannot emphasize this enough. Here are the physiological facts—they are indisputable: The horse is a trickle feeder. He's a grazing animal designed to chew all day long. His chewing produces saliva, which neutralizes the acid that's continually flowing in his stomach. Your stomach produces acid only when you eat; your horse's stomach produces acid constantly, even when the stomach is empty (you see where I am going with this—his stomach should never be empty!). He also needs forage flowing through his digestive tract to exercise those muscles; otherwise the muscles get flabby, which can bring on colic from a weak intestinal tract that torques and intussuscepts. Furthermore, the cecum (hindgut) contains the bacteria responsible for digesting fiber from forage. But its exit and entrance are both at the top! In order for digested material to be pushed to the top, the cecum must be full. Otherwise colic can result from material left at the bottom.

A horse that doesn't have anything to eat will chew on whatever he can—fences, trees, even his own manure. It's pitiful to see. Chewing on non-feedstuffs makes a horse mentally acutely uncomfortable because it goes against his instincts, but physically he is in pain and attempting to resolve it. Discomfort? Pain? Stress! And he's stoic about it. You might look at him and say, "Well, he's calm." Sure, he may look that way but it's an ingrained survival mechanism for horses that are in pain to hide it. In the wild, a horse that shows that he's uncomfortable often gets left behind by the herd to fend for himself against predators. So anatomically and psychologically, the horse has evolved to deal with pain by simply bearing it. Even the pain of an empty stomach.

What happens when you bring this horse some hay? Against the fear of future deprivation and to relieve his stomach discomfort, he inhales it. Then he waits again for his next meal, even while the acid resumes bathing his empty stomach. And it's not only the stomach that is affected. The acid can also damage the entire gastrointestinal tract, even making it all the way down to the hindgut. It can lead to colic and it can lead to laminitis.

I have seen hundreds of cases of horses suffering a laminitis relapse through being placed on a restrictive diet. Here's the scenario: The horse is overweight (maybe even develops laminitis). The well-intentioned veterinarian tells the horse owner, "Put your horse in a dry lot and feed him only a little bit of hay, maybe about 1.5% of his body weight. Give several small hay meals a day, only." And the rest of the time the horse stands there with an empty stomach. The well-intentioned veterinarian has just given the well-intentioned horse owner the worst possible advice because the stress of that leads to cortisol increase, which causes insulin to rise, and when insulin rises you have laminitis—new, recurrent or chronic. This happens over and over again; it is the unfortunate "conventional wisdom" of the horse industry.

I adamantly protest—this practice is not based on sound science.

Recently I read an article that purported to describe how to help the insulin-resistant horse lose weight. Frankly, I was appalled. In the cited study, researchers gave the horse 1.5% of his body weight of soaked hay plus a vitamin/mineral supplement—but nothing to assure protein quality. The horse was allowed one hour per day of so-called grazing—with a muzzle; the rest of the time he was kept in a confined area where he could not move around. So here you've got a horse that's not being allowed to chew, that is not getting enough forage to keep his digestive tract healthy, that is not being allowed to move, that is not getting enough protein, and does he lose weight?

Of course, he loses weight. You would lose weight, too, if you consumed only 1.5% of your body weight and lost muscle mass from inactivity. Let's see, what's 1.5% of, say, 130 pounds? That's 1.95 pounds of food—two pounds of food a day. And let's say you ate those two pounds as lettuce. Of course, you'd lose weight, but you wouldn't be healthy and you would easily gain it back!!

But when a horse loses weight that way, his *metabolic rate slows down so dramatically* that he can't process a larger amount of food without gaining back all the lost weight and more when he returns to eating normally. The most likely next outcome is a laminitis attack.

Now, consider the free choice scenario: First, make sure what the horse is eating is low in NSC and low in calories. Once you know that it's safe, then give your horse all he wants to eat 24/7, and never, ever let him run out—not even for 10 minutes. Very soon, your horse will eat only what he needs. Yes, at first he may overeat because he's so excited, but once he realizes he can walk away and come back and figure out it's no big deal—saying to himself the equivalent of "Yeah, yeah, it's still there"—he will relax. Perceived starvation is no longer a threat and so his hormones start to calm down. His insulin level starts to drop. His body fat starts to be burned for energy rather than being held onto; his body also responds to the hormone, leptin, which tells him he is no longer hungry. He starts to lose weight, and lo and behold, he actually eats less than he did originally because when he has all that he wants, he knows how much he actually needs. Give him a chance to self regulate. A horse whose system is in healthy balance will not naturally overeat. Give him a chance to tell you what he needs.

Forget the dry lot with no hay. Forget the drastically reduced diet. I have seen this horrible damaging protocol again and again. I understand—it is difficult for horse owners to accept anything else. I am not arguing against restricting calories. Of course you have to do that, but you need to do it by giving a low calorie, low sugar/starch hay.

And you need to increase exercise. Exercise decreases insulin resistance. It also builds or helps protect muscle mass (which is metabolically more efficient but which the cushingoid horse is losing) and certainly it directly burns calories which helps your horse lose weight.

Here's an analogy: If I told you that you could lose weight by eating all the chocolate cake and ice cream you wanted and lolling around in a lounge chair all day, you would say that's impossible—even ridiculous—and you'd be right. But if I said that you could lose weight if you chose to eat a lot of low calorie food—if you ate your fill of a variety of vegetables, for example—and got a reasonable amount of exercise, you would think that made sense. That's what I'm telling you to do with your horse. Let him eat low calorie foods, all he wants, because that's what he needs. Help him move around. You get the picture—I hope it makes sense now.

Now that you have a solid understanding of the physiology behind PPID and the best management practices to help your horse stay in maximum good health with the disease, let's go on to your questions.

---

[1] See Appendix B for more on feeding free choice.

[2] Getting your hay analyzed is usually inexpensive and worthwhile, even for as small a quantity as a one-month supply. Send a sample to Equi Analytical Labs (www.equi-analytical.com). They're the horse specialist division of Dairy One. Of course, you can send a sample to a nearby vet school; however, sometimes they take quite a long time to get the results back to you.

[3] Some equine nutritionists recommend adding ESC (ethanol soluble carbohydrates) to percent starch. ESC represents simple sugars and they significantly raise insulin levels, which is what you want to avoid with Cushing's. WSC represents ESC plus fructans. It was thought that fructans are not digested in the foregut and therefore do not contribute to insulin secretion. However, some short chain fructans (oligofructosaccharides) may be digested in the foregut, thereby contributing to blood glucose (and hence, insulin). Therefore, it is best to consider WSC rather than ESC when calculating NSC and its appropriateness for your horse.

[4] If you were to analyze pasture, you would need to use the dry matter levels since pasture is very high in moisture. To make your pasture values more comparable to hay, you can assume an average 93% dry matter and multiply each number in the dry matter column by .93. This will give you a comparable comparison or your pasture to hay with a 93% dry matter level.

[5] See References for information about Dr. Getty's article comparing protein quality in hemp seeds with soybeans.

Questions & Answers

Grazing muzzle for the cushingoid horse. Karen has a cushingoid Morgan mare, 23 years old, that has insulin resistance; the mare's Cushing's condition is being controlled by 2.5 mg of Prascend. Karen is also supplementing vitamin E, selenium, chromium, magnesium. This winter for the first time in years the mare was turned out with other horses (rather than being kept alone in a dry lot) and she was able to eat free choice from a round bale, which she did without becoming obese, as she had been previously. Karen asks if the mare can now safely graze on pasture with the other horses during the summer. They're normally on pasture day and night. Karen has a grazing muzzle she can use with the mare, but she doesn't know if that will restrict the grass enough and she hesitates to keep it on constantly. Karen asks if it's possible that the mare's metabolism has now adjusted, or if socializing and moving around might be helping her.

Answer: Excellent work, Karen! Socializing and moving around both offer lots of benefits in reducing stress and promoting weight loss. So, yes, it is possible to see an adjustment to the mare's metabolism. If her crestiness is no longer there, if she's of normal weight and she doesn't have fat deposits, you can allow some pasture grazing during the safest times of the day[1].

A grazing muzzle is okay for a few hours with this caveat: Grazing muzzles and slow feeders are good things *as long as they don't create frustration*. Frustration is a form of stress, which can cause cortisol to rise, which causes insulin to rise, which can lead to laminitis, so limit grazing muzzles to no more than about three hours; two hours is even better. You must make sure she can drink water and that the water will drain out of the grazing muzzle. Slow feeders are also beneficial but let the horse become accustomed to them.

And you can test your pasture (see endnote 4, page 27), which may give you some peace of mind about the safety of letting her graze. Certainly by the end of June there's a very good chance that the pasture may even be lower in sugar and starch than your hay; I have seen that happen.

Decision to give Prascend. Heidi has a complex situation. She has an Arab-quarter horse mare, 17 years old, that she's owned for many years. Two years ago the mare contracted Lyme disease. She's a fairly easy keeper, but she maintains her weight pretty well with exercise. She is currently getting chia seeds, which is a good source of omega-3s. The mare was on a study of resveratrol, but after this study her ACTH count went from 40 to 50; responding to this, Heidi put her on chasteberry. She is also getting bee pollen, some salt, some herbs, Speedi-beet beet pulp (Emerald Valley), alfalfa hay cubes soaked. She gets hay free choice. The hay is analyzed and is generally low in sugar. Heidi also says the mare goes out on pasture in the summer, coming off pasture at night and going into a dry lot with hay during the daytime. The mare is lame (again) on her right front foot and has had slight colic episodes over the past two months. She's definitely not right and Heidi is very concerned about her. Considering all this, Heidi wonders if she should put the mare on Prascend.

Answer: First, I have to comment about the pasture timing: This is backwards—please see the earlier discussion in this book[2]. Now, more particular answers about this mare... Lyme disease is very debilitating to the nervous system, to the joints, certainly to the immune system, and the treatment can be complicated and difficult. Relating to Cushing's, Lyme's can be problematic in two ways. First, the immune system is already compromised with Cushing's and Lyme disease puts further demands upon it. Second, Lyme disease itself can cause an increase in blood insulin levels, adding to the risk of laminitis. So, good for you, Heidi, for tackling it head-on.

Resveratrol is a very potent antioxidant. It's found in red grapes—so it's also in red wine (although I don't recommend the red wine for your horses!). You mention that the ACTH count was done during the fall; if the starting level of 40 was taken at another time of the year, the 50 count may have been the natural rise we commonly see in ACTH in the fall, and that would mean that the resveratrol probably had little detrimental effect on the ACTH, although leptin levels did go down (which is an indication that she is become less leptin resistant and less likely to overeat). I would have her ACTH levels retested, and test them again in the three month period where they tend to be higher (August, September, and October) so you can compare the two values. A caution about vaccinations, though: If you're planning on having her vaccinated, I would wait until you know if she does have Cushing's and then have that treated before you give her any vaccinations. Once the hormonal cascade is improved by pergolide, her immune system will be better able to handle vaccinations. I do recommend discussing with your veterinarian methods of administering them individually rather than as a bundle.

Have you had your hay actually tested? You said that it was "generally low in sugar," but I'm not sure what that means without numbers. Depending on the test result, you may want to soak your hay if it's not truly and consistently low in NSC.

Preventive medicine. Cindy R. asks, "What is the single most important thing I can do now with my very healthy 5-year-old Arab-quarter horse cross mare to insure that she is not a statistic in her twenties?"

Answer: That is a great question, Cindy. Everything I've mentioned applies, but let me just reiterate the most important points: Make sure that she has the ability to be a horse, and that means grazing on hay or pasture or a combination of both all the time, 24 hours a day, free choice. For more on feeding free choice, please read Appendix B. The gist of this is to give enough hay at night so that there is some left over in the morning. If she runs out of hay, it could have been 10 minutes of 10 hours ago; the point is that you must give more than enough hay at night so that she never runs out. The first night you to this, she is going to overeat so be sure to give her more than she could possibly consume. The next night she will eat a little less and after a few days of free-choice hay, she will finally walk away from it. That is the magic moment! That's when she has gotten the message that she can leave the hay and it will still be there when she returns. It's remarkable how her demeanor will change; she will no longer be anxious to get the hay. She'll be calm about it.

Let me also mention a personal example: I have two horses that always have hay. They also graze on pasture in season. When I bring out hay—even alfalfa—they just kind of look at me as if to say, "That's nice, we'll get to it later." They're just not anxious anymore. Their weight is correct, they are calmer, and they simply trust that food will be available—that potential source of stress is gone. Of course, they eat their alfalfa first because they like it best, but you get the picture.

So getting back to what you should do, Cindy. Test your hay; test your pasture. Make sure that you're providing high quality protein by adding a variety of hay types. Make sure that it is balanced in minerals (typically iron is too high in relation to copper, zinc, and manganese).

Give omega 3s to keep the immune system working properly and insulin levels in balance—this also helps keep the hair and the hooves and the skin healthy. Fresh grass has a ratio of omega 3s to omega 6s of 4:1, which is perfect, so we try to mimic that ratio with supplementation when feeding hay because hay has lost most of its omega 3s. For omega 3s, add some ground flaxseed or chia seeds. Make sure that you're exercising your horse, that she gets plenty of opportunities to move around. Standing in a stall for hours and hours and hours is not only nerve-wracking for your horse but it also can induce colic. It can damage her hooves. It can lead to stress-related oxidative damage and so on. Keep curcumin (the spice turmeric) in your horse's diet even if she doesn't have inflammation; one tablespoon per day is a nice maintenance level for a healthy horse. It's a wonderful antioxidant and promotes health in a variety of ways.[3]

Different forms of pergolide? Catherine asks if there is a particular form of the drug pergolide that is preferable for the insulin resistant horse with Cushing's. Should this horse stay on the medication year round or only through the fall? What is the right dosage to start with?

Answer: Prascend is pergolide in a product made uniform specifically for horses whereas pergolide was compounded for horses from a drug prescribed for Parkinson's disease in humans. Both versions address Cushing's only. You need to control the insulin resistance through diet, through reducing stress, through the environment. Free choice forage feeding is important, with appropriate food. Exercise is very important as well; even hand-walking 10 minutes a day will make a difference. Cushing's medication may only be necessary in the fall, but you must retest to make sure—see my answer to Heidi, above. It really depends on the individual horse and the level of progression. The dosage should be a matter for your veterinarian; usually vets will start with 0.5 mg for a full-sized horse (about 1100 pounds or 500 kg), and then retest and see if that's working well.

Diagnosis criteria for Cushing's. Elisa asks what the definitive diagnosis is for Cushing's.

Answer: If the horse's ACTH tests above 35 pg/ml from November to the following July, then the horse is considered cushingoid. If the level is over 47 taken between August and October, that's usually a red flag, but sometimes the level won't be even that high and the horse will start exhibiting symptoms, so you want to feed the horse as though he is cushingoid with all the things that I mentioned.

Exercise for a horse with Cushing's. Elisa asks what the proper role is, if any, for exercise for the horse with Cushing's.

Answer: Exercise is wonderful as long as your horse feels like moving. If your horse is, for example, laminitic, then you don't want to force him to move. But for the insulin-resistant horse or the cushingoid horse exhibiting signs of insulin resistance, exercise is helpful. There are distinct benefits: It burns calories; it builds muscle (metabolically more active than fat); it increases the insulin receptors on the cell membranes to make them more insulin sensitive, allowing body fat to be burned for energy. As body fat declines, leptin resistance also diminishes, allowing your horse to respond to leptin through a reduced appetite.

Testing options for horse on pergolide. Paula wants to know if it is possible to utilize any of the PPID testing options if the horse is already being treated with pergolide. Paula started pergolide when the horse was diagnosed as insulin resistant but was not successful in preventing laminitis.

Answer: You can still do other testing options, but the best thing to do, frankly, is retest the ACTH to see if the levels have changed since starting the pergolide. Pergolide might not be the appropriate treatment, actually. Remember that metabolic syndrome, which has nothing to do with the pituitary gland, is manifested as insulin resistance so the horse could be diagnosed with insulin resistance and not have Cushing's. Nevertheless, if the horse has the Cushing's symptoms I mentioned earlier, then you may assume that there's a likelihood that the horse is developing Cushing's, especially if he does have metabolic syndrome and is getting up in years. I would definitely watch the stress level and retest the ACTH.

Cushing's prevention for the older horse. Leslie adopted two Spanish mustangs, one 22 and one 16. She thought the oldest might have Cushing's, but blood tests were negative. She would like to prevent this disease in both horses. So she wants to know what types of food she should give them—should it be low in starch and low in sugar, should it be a senior feed, and can she put both horses on the same diet?

Answer: First a comment about the blood tests: Be cautious about them—false negative (and positive) results are not uncommon. If the symptoms that prompted the blood tests persist, consider retesting. Regardless, the goal is to slow the progression. All feed for these horses should be low in starch and low in sugar. Be aware that senior feeds typically have some molasses which, remember, you want to avoid. Triple Crown Senior has an NSC of about 12% which is likely low enough, but there are feeds with even lower NSC levels[4]. You can put both of them on the same feed; that's not a problem. Your older horse may benefit from additional attention to vitamin C and digestive enzymes. Please take a look at the book on Aging Horse, part of this *Spotlight on Equine Nutrition Series.*

The thing about feeding any product that comes out of a bag is that you must feed it according to directions in order for the horse to get all the feed's stated vitamin and mineral supplementation. If you don't, then you're going to have to "supplement the supplement," so to speak. Instead, you might just want to feed something basic like soaked beet pulp (drain off and discard the water) plus maybe some alfalfa hay pellets, and then add a good vitamin and mineral supplement. If the horse is predominantly on hay, then add a ground flaxseed-based supplement that has high amounts of vitamin E and other antioxidants to replace everything that's lost in hay; the one I recommend is Glanzen Complete which is a custom product available on my website or directly from HorseTech.

You also said, Leslie, that you have a special treat dispenser which they love; I expect they do, but what matters is what you put in it. You currently use timothy cubes (those are good); apple chunks (only a very small amount); apple-flavored cookies and horse candies that are pure sugar—no, those are not a good idea. You can use alfalfa cubes, you can use alfalfa pellets. Apple *peels* (not the actual fruit) contain a substance called ursolic acid, which actually reduces insulin resistance.

SmartPak SmartDigest. Leslie asks specifically about a supplement called SmartPak SmartDigest and whether there are better supplements for digestion.

Answer: SmartPak SmartDigest is a very nice probiotic and digestive aid. It's certainly worthwhile if your horse has any digestive problems or is prone toward ulcers. If your horse has ulcers, consider using Starting Gate (SBS Equine Products). In addition to the Glanzen Complete (or Glanzen Lite Complete for a horse with some weight issues), you want to add some magnesium. There's a product called Carb-X (Med-Vet Pharmaceuticals) which has magnesium and lipoic acid; Quiessence (Foxden) is another good one that's not as potent as Carb-X but it doesn't sound like you need something really, really potent. Magnesium, psyllium pellets, CurOST (Nouvelle Veterinary) which contains curcumin—these are all available at a lot of different places as well as my website.

Uncontrolled appetite. Cindy D. has a 29 year old horse with Cushing's and a voracious appetite. He's a tall, lean quarter horse without fat deposits, but prone to laminitis that is secondary to his Cushing's disease. When she first had him tested, his insulin was off the charts. All signs confirmed his Cushing's diagnosis: She did a cortisol rhythm test that showed that he was cushingoid, and the test results were borne out by symptoms like a long hair coat (he requires body clipping three times a year). His ACTH levels came back four times higher than the upper normal range, and he's been on pergolide for two years. He's been getting 1.5 mg but the veterinarian doubled the dose and plans to retest. He has a ravenous appetite despite being fed grass hay free choice. He gets Triple Crown Senior to maintain his weight. In the winter his behavior was acutely disruptive; he hollered every time he saw her, banging on fence gates and knocking around buckets in his impatience to eat. He just couldn't be satiated, no matter what. She installed an automatic feeder, to have Triple Crown pellets dispensed during the night; in total he was getting about six meals during a 24-hour period along with plenty of hay. However, he turned up his nose at the hay most of the time and wait for the pelleted feed. Cindy asks what is causing this extreme hunger. She also asked about giving this horse chasteberry at very high levels.

Answer: The likely cause of this extreme hunger is leptin resistance. Leptin is secreted from fat cells and normally tells the horse that he is satisfied and appetite subsides. With leptin resistance, the satiety center in the brain does not respond and the horse continues to overeat. Leptin will be high (which you may want to have tested). The only way to reduce leptin resistance is to burn body fat, so exercise is likely your only option.

Another contributing factor to his appetite is the fact that his pituitary gland has hypertrophied (enlarged) so much it is putting pressure on the hypothalamus which controls the hunger satiation, so he's not able to get the signal that he's no longer hungry. He may also be diabetic. As insulin resistance gets worse and worse and worse, the pancreas cells can actually die out and eventually stop producing insulin, so although it's not very common, he could develop type 1 diabetes (which could account for his leanness since body fat is burned when glucose cannot get into the cells). This is an insulin-dependent diabetes, which means he would require insulin injections because the body can't produce enough of it, and therefore the glucose cannot get into the tissues. So it may be worth having him tested; type 1 diabetes would be indicated by very high levels of glucose and low levels of insulin.

I am concerned about his rejecting his hay and waiting to eat until he can have more pellets; this means that he's probably not chewing enough (remember, saliva is the natural antacid), and that can possibly damage his digestive tract. Giving him hay only would be better certainly but I understand your perspective. I would choose a different pelleted feed, however, one completely without molasses.

About chasteberry: Feeding it may cut down on the amount of pergolide that the horse needs but I really think for this horse, Cushing's has progressed so far that only more potent antioxidants would help slow the progression. Curcumin is very important, plus high amounts of vitamin E and high amounts of vitamin C, all of which he needs anyway at his age. And if you suspect an ulcer, Starting Gate lecithin/apple pectin granules are worthwhile.

Edema. Carol has a 24-year-old Morgan that grows a long winter coat that's slow to shed. He's ridden two or three times a week, has 24/7 turnout, and unlimited hay. His weight is good, his health is fine. He has been getting Safe Choice feed but is switching to Safe Choice Special Care (both, Nutrena). In the winter he's less active and he retains fluid in his sheath. Exercise helps clear it up but Carol wants to know if the fluid retention is related to the Cushing's disease. And what are the recommendations?

Answer: Edema is controlled by the hypothalamus. If the pituitary gland has hypertrophied (enlarged), then it pushes up against the hypothalamus, which can disrupt its ability to regulate water balance, and that can lead to edema. Another thing that comes to mind is that in the wintertime he may not be drinking enough water, which is very common because horses don't like ice cold water. So make sure—if you're not already doing this—that the water is heated. Make sure, too, that you give him salt year round. He should have an ounce (two tablespoons or 30 ml) of table salt or the equivalent per day. And check the salt level in his feed. Also—and this is important—neither Safe Choice (with approximately 22% NSC) nor Safe Choice Special Care (a bit lower at 15% NSC) are truly safe. Choose something that's even lower in NSC—see the list I mentioned previously, on page XXX.

Thyro-L and the laminitic horse. Donna has a 13 year old horse that's laminitic. After an acute episode during which he was on Previcox, he's now better. He gets Cetyl M and he eats grass hay from a big bale. He gets a pound of LMF Super Supplement (LMF Feeds) and two scoops of Thyro-L (Vet-A-Mix) each day. Is all of this appropriate?

Answer: Let me address the Thyro-L first. Hypothyroidism is not related to Cushing's yet vets often give Thyro-L because it speeds up the metabolic rate and helps the horse lose weight. But it does damage the thyroid gland, eventually rendering it virtually inactive. So if he's been on Thyro-L for no more than about three or four months, then I'd recommend that you start weaning him off of it. If he's been on it for a year or more, then the damage may already be done and he may need to be on it for the rest of his life.

LMF Super Supplement is not appropriate for your horse. Although the first ingredient listed is soy, the next three are cereal grains: whole wheat, ground corn, and barley. In fact, I never feed corn at all to horses; it is poorly digested and can lead to cecal acidosis—a cause of laminitis. These grains make this supplement high in starch which increases insulin, and that could lead to a laminitis relapse. So absolutely, don't feed that high amount of starch. Switch to a vitamin/mineral supplement that does not contain grains. I like Glanzen Lite Complete because it's ground flaxseed-based. Or choose High Point Grass (HorseTech) daily supplement designed to complement grass hay diets, and then add some Nutra-Flax or Nutra-Chia (both, HorseTech) for omega 3s.

Pergolide and arthritis. Patti has a 24-year-old horse that's very sensitive to pergolide. He was on 0.5 mg of plain pergolide and he wouldn't eat so she lowered the dose and now she's starting to work him back up to the original level. He's also developed mild arthritis and it's very painful, yet she has changed nothing except increasing his dose. Her veterinarian says that arthritis pain has been reported with pergolide but only in rare instances. The horse is on whole foods with no sugar. He gets steamed hay, which reduces the sugar by 3%. He wears a muzzle for five hours. She hand walks him for 20-30 minutes a day and he's doing very well. Patti asks if the arthritis reaction will wear off or continue.

Answer: Yes, it is possible for pergolide to exacerbate arthritis pain. In addition to decreasing ACTH, pergolide decreases other POMC peptides including one called beta-endorphin, and endorphins relieve pain. So you may have to experiment with the dosage. You may also need to give a buteless preparation to increase the horse's comfort; I like Stop the Pain (Cox Veterinary Laboratory) or SuPer Substitute (has no sugar). Both of these are herbal preparations that work very well along with turmeric; they can help with arthritis pain dramatically. (I speak about this from personal experience with my own horse.) Make sure the horse gets hay free choice. The muzzle for five hours is a little bit long, so if you could reduce it to three that would be better.

Another reason for arthritis is inadequate zinc or copper; that can cause joint damage. Since steaming the hay may somewhat deplete those minerals, you want to make sure that the diet contains a supplement for vitamins and minerals. Whole foods are great in addition to supplementation if all he's getting is hay but they do not take the place of supplementation—only fresh grass can do that because your horse consumes 40 to 50 lbs of grass each day. Hay is missing so many things, you couldn't possibly feed enough whole foods to replace the vitamins and minerals in the equivalent amount of fresh grass. Keep that in mind.

Diet for Cushing's compared to one for insulin resistance. Bonnie asks how the Cushing's diet differs from the insulin resistant diet. Her horse is an easy keeper, "cresty neck and all." She feeds something called Barn

Bag (Life Data Labs), plus timothy pellets, shredded beet pulp, and free-choice coastal hay. The diet is low in NSC but she doesn't see any change in his neck crestiness. Any suggestions?

Answer: The Cushing's diet and the insulin resistant diet are really not a whole lot different. What differs is the underlying reason for each condition. Insulin resistance is caused by genetic reasons or obesity; a Cushing's horse is insulin resistant secondarily as a result of the pituitary gland problem.

Barn Bag is a good supplement that you can continue feeding, but you probably need to add a little more magnesium—do the calculations to get the magnesium up to the level of half the amount of calcium that's in the diet, including the hay (so have your hay analyzed). Psyllium is also worth giving, about a third of a cup (80 ml) per meal. And you don't need both timothy pellets and beet pulp for carriers; Stick with timothy pellets. Beet pulp adds calories (and iron), and that's not what you want. Maybe add extra omega 3s from a ground flaxseed product such as Nutra-Flax. And by the way, do not use Omega Horseshine. Omega Horseshine is a very popular ground flaxseed product, but it contains oats, and starch is certainly not what you want to feed your easy keeper.

So, in summary, increase the insulin lowering propensity of the diet by adding magnesium, psyllium, and omega 3s and that will help with the neck crestiness. Of course, he also needs to exercise. All of that ought to make a very big difference.

Stocking up (edema, swelling, or fill) in the right hind. Paula's mare is insulin resistant and apparently cushingoid. The horse frequently or sporadically has some fill in her right hind, and that is typically a precursor to a laminitic episode. Paula wonders what is causing this stocking up. There is no increase in digital pulse. The horse gets salt via a salt block.

Answer: Any time there is a water imbalance, as evidenced by stocking up (edema), that is an indication of the pituitary gland getting so large that it's pressing up against the hypothalamus, preventing the hypothalamus from regulating water. Make sure that she's getting enough salt to encourage her to drink more water, so it will flush out all of the salt and the retained water. She may not be getting enough salt from her salt block; if she's licking the salt block, fine, but the salt block typically irritates the horse's tongue and most horses don't like it enough to get adequate salt (they need about an ounce per day). I recommend you also offer granulated salt free choice, or you can add about a tablespoon (15 ml) of salt to each of her two meals.

Edema can also be a result of inflammation that already exists in that hoof. So, although the laminitis may appear to come second to the swelling, it may be that the swelling is actually due to the early stages of laminitis. Therefore, when you see swelling, consider it a possible sign that she is developing laminitis.

You may want to do some cryotherapy, which is placing the hoof in some ice water to calm down any inflammation.

I would also increase vitamin E and vitamin C. Add some CoQ10, which is a potent antioxidant—give about 600 mg, which ought to help reduce free radical formation. Add some turmeric as well, which you can buy in bulk at any store that sells whole foods, or look into CurOst supplements available on my website.

Paula clarifies: The horse doesn't always develop laminitis in the hind foot where the swelling occurs. She can also develop laminitis in her front feet. Paula wonders is this is a hindgut issue.

Answer: **There are two different forms of laminitis and the distinction is important because it determines the choice of treatment.**

Laminitis that affects the hindgut is usually due to feeding large amounts of starch or forage that is high in fructans, that reach the hindgut. It is not the same cause of laminitis as endocrine-related laminitis, which is where feeding high starch levels causes insulin to rise. Certainly you want to pay attention to the hindgut bacteria and to reduce blood insulin levels, make sure you're not feeding anything starchy. Make sure that she's getting a good pro- and pre-biotic to keep the hindgut healthy. Syn-

Biotic EQ (Med-Vet) and SmartDigest (SmartPak) are very good. For more on this, please refer to my book, *Laminitis: A Scientific and Realistic Approach.*

Icelandic with laminitis. Brenda has an overweight Icelandic that has laminitis. Her vet says that Brenda should severely restrict the mare's hay. Brenda knows this isn't right, and asks for advice.

Answer: Icelandics are not truly horses – they are ponies and therefore they are not only prone toward insulin resistance, but also, if not allowed to graze, they can develop a condition called hyperlipemia. This happens when the body uses fat as an energy source because forage is restricted. It is a very dangerous condition. Therefore, allow her to graze on the low NSC hay that you have available. And fill in the gaps with good vitamin/mineral supplement such as High Point for grass diets. You can add a small amount of Nutra Flax for additional omega 3s (say one scoop per day). And then give her CarbX to help further lower blood insulin levels. Finally, curcumin (CurOst supplements or turmeric) will ease the inflammation both from the laminitis as well as from the obesity.

Supplementing with whole foods. Patti likes to supplement vitamins and minerals using whole foods. Is this sufficient?

Answer: Whole foods are very different than supplements. Grass, for example, is a perfect whole food. And the horse eats many, many pounds of it each day. If the horse does not have access to grass, and is fed hay instead, it would take an impractically large amount of a whole food to replace what is in the grass that he's missing. For example, one orange couldn't possibly replace all of the vitamin C found in 40 lbs or more of grass. So, if you want to replace the vitamin C found in grass, you would have to feed a vitamin C supplement. Giving your horse an orange would not come close to filling in the gap. So, whole food supplements are wonderful to feed to boost an already nutritious diet (fresh, living grass) but cannot be expected to bring a hay-only diet up to the same level.

Summary

Let me summarize what we've discussed.

Our goal is to reduce oxidative stress which will help to slow down the progression of Cushing's. You cannot prevent the progression entirely but you can significantly hinder its development. To reduce stress, let your horse be a horse. Feed his muscles and his immune system, make sure he gets quality protein. Provide antioxidants. Provide low-calorie, low-NSC hay. Exercise him. Reduce inflammation through antioxidants and curcumin and reduction of body fat. And then use pergolide if necessary, depending on how advanced his Cushing's situation is. And test and retest because the situation is dynamic and very fluid.

It's a pleasure to present information to such very conscientious horse owners who are eager to learn more. We're always learning. It's a never-ending journey.

---

[1] See page 16.

[2] See page 16.

[3] See References for information about Dr. Getty's article on curcumin.

[4] See page 20 for names of lower NSC feeds.

Appendix A
Antioxidants, the Unsung Heroes

Antioxidant. The word implies that it *goes against* something involving oxygen. But oxygen is necessary for life, so why need something contrary to it? Truth is that oxidation of carbohydrates, proteins, and fats within your horse's cells is an ongoing process and is necessary for the production of energy to fuel work, maintenance, and normal metabolic pathways. As a result of oxidation, free radicals are formed – many thousands of them each day. And they have an important function in destroying bacteria and viruses, serving a role in protecting your horse's immune function. But if the horse is experiencing physical or mental stressors (e.g., forage restriction, strenuous exercise, illness, pain, traveling, stall confinement, etc.), the level of free radical formation can overpower the body's ability to counteract them, leading to the destruction of normal, healthy cells.

A free radical is an unbalanced molecule; it is missing an electron. To ease this "discomfort," the free radical will steal an electron from balanced cells, starting a chain reaction of "electron stealing" from cell to cell, leading to tissue damage, disease, and accelerated aging.

The antioxidant is the hero – it stops this damaging rampage in its tracks by giving of itself – donating its own electron to the free radical. Since the antioxidant is now unstable itself, *it is important to include several antioxidants in the diet to ensure that the unstable one is neutralized and able to function again.*

Appendix B
What It Means to Feed Free Choice

The horse's digestive tract is designed to have forage flowing through it every minute of every day. At night, too!

The intestines are made of muscles and require forage to keep them exercised and conditioned, in order to assure efficient nutrient processing and prevent colic. The cecum, with its exit at the top, must be full so that food matter can be pushed up and out to continue through the digestive process. Furthermore, the horse's stomach continuously secretes acid, even when empty; horses need to chew to produce saliva, a natural antacid. Running out of hay is physically painful and mentally stressful, virtually assuring the formation of an ulcer. But that's not all – the hormonal response created by forage restriction tells the horse to hold on to body fat, creating a weight management nightmare and making it very difficult for the overweight horse to lose weight.

The solution: Feed your horse the way he was designed to eat.

Step 1: *Know what you are feeding.* Test your hay and/or pasture. Especially when feeding overweight horses, the forage should be low in non-structural carbohydrates (NSC)—NSC should be less than 12% on an as-sampled basis. And it should be low in calories (known as digestible energy) at no more than 0.88 Mcals/lb on an as-sampled basis.

Step 2: Once you have determined the forage is appropriate to feed, **feed it free choice**. Always have forage available, 24/7. The hay should never run out, not even for 10 minutes. And not just during the day—nighttime is important, too.

Then be patient, step back and watch your horse do what comes naturally. Give the process approximately 2-3 weeks; most horses take less time, some take up to a month. At first he will overeat, but once he understands that the hay is always there, he will walk away – that's the magic moment! He will calm down, eat more slowly, and self-regulate his intake, eating only what his body needs to maintain condition.

Allow your horse to tell you how much he needs. He may even eat less than before because running out of hay is no longer an issue. Trust this will happen. Soon, your horse's weight will adjust into the normal, healthy range, his behavior will be more natural and steady, and his health will be more vibrant.

References

Andrews, F.M., and Frank, N., 2009. Pathology of metabolic-related conditions: Equine Cushing's disease (Pituitary pars intermedia dysfunction). www.ker.com/library/advances/429.pdf

Daubner, S.C., Le, T., and Wang, S., 2011. Tyrosine hydroxylase and regulation of dopamine synthesis. *Archives of Biochemistry and Biophysics, 508*(1), 1-12.

Getty, J.M, 2013. Commercial feeds for the IR horse. *Horse Journal, 20*(1), January, 1-6.

Getty, J.M. February, 2013. Consider curcumin for joint inflammation. Library, www.gettyequinenutrition.com.

Getty, J.M. April, 2013. Hemp seeds rival soybeans in protein quality. Library, www.gettyequinenutrition.com.

Kellon, E.M., 2000. Herbal offers hope for Cushing's syndrome. *Horse Journal, 7,* 3-7.

McFarlane, D., Donaldson, M.T., Saleh, T.M., and Cribb, A.E., 2003. The role of dopaminergic neurodegeneration in equine pituitary pars intermedia dysfunction (Equine Cushing's disease), *49th Annual convention of the American Association of Equine Practitioners,* New Orleans, Louisiana.

McGowan, T.W., Pinchbeck, G.P., and McGowan, C.M., 2013. Prevalence, risk factors and clinical signs predictive for equine pituitary pars intermedia dysfunction in aged horses. *Equine Veterinary Journal, 45*(1), 74-79.

Miller, Grant, 2013. Cushing's disease: A slow, silent, formidable foe. *Horse Journal, 20(*9), September, 1-5.

Mayo, J.L., 1998. Black cohosh and chasteberry: Herbs valued by women for centuries. *Clinical Nutrition Insights, 6*(15).

Nielsen, B.D., Vick, M.M., and Dennis, P.M. 2012. A potential link between insulin resistance and iron overload disorder in browsing rhinoceroses investigated through the use of an equine model. *Journal of Zoo and Wildlife Medicine, 43*(3), S61-S65.

Oke, S. 2012. Similar but different: Equine Cushing's disease and EMS. *The Horse, www.thehorse.com,* #29230.

Shannon, J.J. M., Nichols, J.L., Bowman, J.G.P., and Hatfield, P.G. 2011. Psyllium lowers blood glucose and insulin concentrations in horses. *Journal of Equine Veterinary Science, 31,* 160-165.

Tess, T.M., et.al., 2013. Effects of omega-3 fatty acid supplementation on insulin sensitivity in horses. *Journal of Equine Veterinary Science, 33*(6), 446-453.

van Epps, A.W., and Pollitt, C.C., 2006. Equine laminitis induced with oligofructose. *Journal of Veterinary Medicine, 38*(3), 203-208.

CPSIA information can be obtained
at www.ICGtesting.com
Printed in the USA
LVHW021444090821
694887LV00004B/172